My Bipolar Life

Phyllis Kraps

Dedication

To my sister Marsha

*Your love and guidance have made me
into the woman I am today.*

Acknowledgement

I am blessed with family and friends who believe in me. They have encouraged me to follow my dreams and write this book. I could not have completed this task without their love and support. I am truly grateful.

A special thank you to Mrs. Abbey and Glenda Holland for taking the time out of their busy schedules to proofread and edit my book. They truly inspired me.

About the Author:

Phyllis Kraps was born and raised in Northeast Ohio. She is the youngest of three.

Her life long career was in the accounting field. Throughout her career she struggled with addiction, autoimmune diseases and mental illness. Despite those difficulties she advanced her career. In 1998 she started up her own company, Office Solutions Unlimited. It was an instant success. She eventually sold it in 2013.

Her other passion in life is helping others during times of struggle. Her lifelong goal is to inspire those who have faced similar issues to overcome and thrive.

She is a retired widow who lives a quiet life with her larger-than-life dog and her quirky cat.

Contents

My Bipolar Life

By Phyllis Kraps

My name is Phyllis Kraps. Yes, that really is my name and if you say it fast enough it sounds like full of crap. Funny, huh? Now that we got that settled, I would like to share with you why I am writing this memoir. I promise you it will be short and sweet. I am a straight and to the point kind of gal.

This year I turned sixty and finally accepted the fact that I have bipolar disorder. Some people are slow learners. I guess where this subject is concerned, I am one of them. Thirty years ago, I was diagnosed with bipolar disorder and that is when I was introduced to the term. What I heard was, "You are crazy!" And

I was not having any of that. Who wants to be stuck with that kind of stigma? I sure as hell didn't.

I have been seen by many psychiatrists and therapists throughout my life. What they were saying was broken, I thought was normal. What's wrong with running on high energy? I call that ambition. What's wrong with racing thoughts? That's just how my mind works. What's wrong with working on a project for two days in a row with no sleep? That's just perseverance. What if I am loud? I am just animated. I've been hyper all my life. I'm just different, that's all. I like who I am. I'm not crazy, the rest of the world is.

I decided to ignore the diagnosis and run like the wind. The funny thing about running is if you do not stop you eventually crash and burn. I crashed and burned five times throughout my life.

This landed me in several different Psych Units. You would have thought that after the 1st or 2nd time; I would have believed the doctors. As I said, I was a slow learner.

Denial is a funny thing especially when you have other issues involved like PTSD or my general anxiety disorder. Many of my symptoms overlapped with bipolar disorder. I was able to accept my PTSD diagnosis because it manifested from the trauma I endured. I was unable to accept a mental defect like bipolar disorder. I am not crazy!

For many years I controlled my bipolar disorder (or so I thought) then it got to the point that it was controlling me. It took the fifth time in a Psychiatric Hospital to finally open my eyes to the fact I have a mental disorder and guess what? I am not crazy!

The reason why I am writing this book is to get it into the hands of all of those who have been diagnosed with bipolar. They can read for themselves that they are not alone in their struggles and they are definitely not crazy. Maybe, just maybe those who are fighting off their diagnosis can get on the road to recovery a lot sooner than I did and stop the Madness!

By the way, what is Bipolar?

I never fully understood what the hell Bipolar was until recently. As I said before, when I heard the term, I just heard, CRAZY! So, I ran like the wind.

I finally decided to research this mental disorder. Boy, was I surprised by my findings. According to the NIH.gov website, approximately 2.8% of the adult US Population has bipolar disorder. That's several million people. I thought I was the only one dealing with this disorder.

Experts believe that bipolar disorder is a chemical imbalance in the brain, however, the actual cause is unknown. Researchers are trying to find a genetic link to see if you can inherit the disorder from a parent. Some research has found people with Bipolar have family members with the same or other mental disorders.

Some experts suggest that bipolar can be triggered by a traumatic event. I was molested at seven years old, raped at fifteen years old, and raped a second time when I was eighteen years old. The experts could be right about being triggered by trauma. I don't know for sure.

There are three types of bipolar disorder.

☒ Bipolar I – which consists of severe mood episodes from Mania to Depression that last at least 7 days. Symptoms can be so severe that hospitalization is necessary

- ☒ Bipolar II – which consists of mild forms of mood swings from hypomania to Depression
- ☒ Cyclothymia – which consists of brief mood swings that are not excessive or long-lasting

I was diagnosed with Bipolar I. How did I get so lucky? Huh!

Now that I know the different types of this mental disorder and now you know the different types. Let us take a look at what mania and depression consists of. I have experienced all of the following behaviors throughout my life. Talk about a rude awakening. The writing on the wall was staring me in the face in black and white.

Mania looks like this:

- ☒ Overly excited or extremely happy
- ☒ Excessive or rapid talking

- ☒ Sleepless nights
- ☒ Increased sexual drive
- ☒ Lack of Concentration
- ☒ Overly Confident

While in a Manic state you may:

- ☒ Abuse drugs and/or alcohol
- ☒ Act out sexually out of character
- ☒ Spend too much cash
- ☒ Have anger outbursts or act aggressively
- ☒ Become excessively active
- ☒ Take extreme risks
- ☒ Having poor judgment or making poor decisions

Depression looks like this:

- ☒ Deep sadness
- ☒ Excessive weepiness
- ☒ Excessive fatigue
- ☒ Feelings of hopelessness & unworthiness

- ☒ Lack of concentration
- ☒ Restless, irritable, and discontent

While in a Depressed state you may:

- ☒ Sleep excessively
- ☒ Become unmotivated
- ☒ Overeat or not eat at all
- ☒ Withdraw from family & friends & social settings
- ☒ Stop self-care like brushing your teeth or taking a shower
- ☒ Think about or try to commit suicide or want to die

I also found out that people with Bipolar have different thought processes:

- ☒ Racing thoughts – where your mind just won't shut off
- ☒ Bouncing from one idea to the next & to the next & to the next, etc.

- ☒ Excessive talking – not allowing another to get a word in edgewise
- ☒ Obsess past situations that you can't let go of

Who knew?! Again, all of the above applied to my thought process before getting treatment. My behavior was normal for me and I didn't see anything wrong with that. I could never understand why some people would have issues with my behavior. This is just the way I am.

I learned a lot about myself during my research. What I got out of all the research is that people with Bipolar live in a world of extremes. Everybody has the same feelings and emotions; those of us with Bipolar just can't help but take our behavior over the edge.

My Mania Life

All that research on bipolar disorder made my head spin. Reflecting on my life seeing my manic behavior hit me hard. I saw how off the charts I was throughout my life. It wasn't pretty.

As a teenager, I was loud, obnoxious, overly excitable, constantly talking, and my mind would not shut off. I had extreme mood swings and I couldn't sit still. You may say all teenagers are like that but I was always getting in trouble at school and home for my behavior. I just couldn't help it. I'd try to reel it in but I really couldn't control my wildness.

At home when I was wound up, I would either frantically clean the house or rock in a rocking chair. That sounds normal, right? Well, my rocking was hard and fast and lasted for hours on end which caused me to break many rocking chairs in our household. That pissed my parents off many times! But cleaning and rocking kept me out of trouble for the most part.

At school my outlet was sports; I played volleyball & basketball. There I was able to get loud and excitable but sometimes I'd go too far, especially in basketball. I'd rough up the other players on the opposing team as often as I could get away with it. I don't know why I would get so aggressive. It just felt good to me.

The best time in school when I didn't feel out of place or get in trouble for being so loud and hyper was when I was a cheerleader. I loved it. I could scream at the top of my lungs and jump around for hours. It helped me a lot during those years.

What also helped me a lot in my teenage years were drugs and alcohol. When I smoked my first joint, I felt peace inside for the first time. At that point, I was hooked. You see, on the inside, I was like a volcano ready to erupt. Then I added alcohol to the mix. It had a calming effect on me as well. I never understand how I could drink more than most kids my age and not feel the effects as much as they did.

By the time I was sixteen, I drank and/or smoked dope almost every day. I liked how it made me feel. I wasn't as anxious or as loud and my thoughts slowed down. I still went to school every day and maintained a B average for the most part, so I didn't think there was anything wrong with my behavior. There were a couple of times I embarrassed myself while drunk. Thank God they didn't have Facebook back then.

By the time I turned eighteen, I graduated with heavier drugs. I kind of missed the manic side of me by using pot and alcohol that is when I added speed to the mix. I remember getting to the point of taking ten hits a day and then doing quaaludes at night to go to sleep. I guess I was self-medicating at that point.

My life consisted of going to bars and parties. Ups and downs for almost a year. I had all these big plans for my life but I couldn't commit to anything other than the next party.

I couldn't commit to guys either. Inside I never felt good enough or worthy enough to have a relationship with anyone. I was always moody and I always found a way to mess it up somehow. One minute I was happy, the next I couldn't stand to be around them. I would break it off if they got too close or if I got too close to them. If they knew what was truly going on inside of me, they would have thought I was crazy. My dad always said I was.

I was nineteen years old when I went cold turkey from drugs and alcohol. I was living with my sister at the time. I quit because I had a close call with the mix of speed, Quaaludes, and painkillers. I will never forget how sick I was. For several days I had nightmares & cold sweats. I couldn't eat or drink anything without getting sick. My sister eventually took me to the hospital. They gave me a shot for pain, a shot for nausea, and a forty-five-minute IV and sent me home. That helped me get past the pain of withdrawals.

I wound up going to my family physician the next day. He knew I needed help. He sent me to a drug and alcohol rehab counseling center for outpatient care. I never abused drugs again. At that point, I started to control my drinking.

I truly wanted my life to be better than it was at that point. I decided it was time to settle down, get married, and have a family. I thought that if I had a stable home and a good man in my life that would fix me.

It took me a couple of years to find Mr. Right. It was a fast & furious romance, just like everything else in my life. We got married six months after we met. He was fun and exciting and stable just what I needed.

When the honeymoon was over, I grew restless, irritable, and discontent and it was all his fault. So, I thought. Two people who drank as we did was a sign of disaster waiting to happen. Our marriage could have been defined as extreme highs and lows. The good times were the best, but the bad times were the worst. We were both verbally & physically abusive when we fought. It was truly toxic. We spent half of the time hurting one another and the other half trying to make up for all the wrongs we both did. The funny thing was that I never doubted his love for me. We just didn't know how to communicate. I finally got off the roller coaster ride after five years. I didn't leave because I didn't love him, I left because I couldn't live that way anymore.

When I left, I had all these grand ideas about how I was going to make my life better. I got a job and found an apartment within a month. I was on my way. Then I had this bright idea that it was time for me to start living and having some fun. The drinking, the parties, and the men became my outlet, yet again.

This lasted about three years. I'd party all night and go to work still drunk. I'd go out dancing four nights out of the week and still go to work. I'd drink and drive and think nothing of it. Men would come and go and I was happy about that. I ran up credit card debts knowing I would never be able to pay them off. I was living the dream.

I was in my late twenties when I started noticing most of my friends were getting married, buying houses, having children, and having careers. They had responsibilities and I ran from mine. I started to feel like something was wrong with me but I didn't do anything to change the situation. I wasn't happy when I was married and I sure wasn't happy being single. The feeling of worthlessness was sinking in deep. That definitely wasn't what I thought my life would have been like at this stage of the game. But I couldn't get off of the merry-go-round.

I couldn't get my life on track because I could never stop long enough to make a plan and follow through. I found myself miserable and out of control. Drinking controlled my mania for most of my earlier life.

I finally quit drinking in 1991 after I got my first DUI. I didn't go to jail thank God. I had to spend a weekend at the Holiday Inn for drug & alcohol counseling. I called it my holiday jail. During one of the sessions, they had a speaker who was a member of Alcoholics Anonymous. He told his story about his drinking career which made me open my eyes to my drinking career. I realized then I had a problem. The day I got home from my holiday jail I decided to get sober and went to my first AA meeting.

If you are not familiar with a recovery program, let me explain it in a nutshell. There are 12 steps to recovery that you have to follow to stay sober. It was not easy but it changed my life.

During the first six months of sobriety, I struggled with anxiety, racing thoughts, severe mood swings, sleepless nights, and feelings of unworthiness but I stayed sober. I wanted so badly to make a better life for myself. But I was struggling.

Things began to change when I finally took the fourth step in my sobriety by taking a fearless moral inventory of myself. It wasn't pretty but I learned to forgive myself and made amends to the people I hurt during my drinking career. I learned how to communicate with others by being honest and not running away from my problems. The people in Alcoholics Anonymous taught me that. I will forever be grateful to them and for the 12 Steps. They taught me step by step how to live life again without a drink.

When you get sober and stop running you have to face the destruction of your past to move forward. I faced what I did to others. But what about the destruction from others that was inflicted upon me? I was left with the after-effects of being molested and raped from my past like trust issues and fear of intimacy. I never dealt with them. I drank them away in the past. Boy did those issues cause problems in my sobriety.

I was trying to live a normal life without alcohol. The trouble started when I started dating. I didn't trust men. I had trouble with intimacy and quite frankly I never had sex sober.

The first time I wigged out (that's what I called it) and wound up in a psych unit I was about a year sober. I had just broken up with my boyfriend. I started having nightmares of my previous rapes. I had sleepless nights. I began to get paranoid and I was crippled with fear. I was ready to jump out of my skin. I could not relax. After about the third sleepless night for some reason, I got in my car and started to drive around aimlessly. I drove and drove. I got lost in Cleveland. My car broke down and I began to walk home. Unfortunately, I was barefoot and had no idea where to go. I don't know why I didn't try to find a phone. Of course, we didn't have cell phones back then. I just kept walking. I walked all night. Sometime in the morning, I wound up in a neighborhood. My feet were getting torn up from all the walking. I needed to do something. I decided to knock on someone's door and ask them for shoes and directions. I was very happy that a sweet old lady answered the door and gave me a pair of flip-flops and pointed me on my way. I got to the highway and hitchhiked to a store. They were kind enough to let me use a phone. I called a friend of mine to come to pick me up. I don't remember her picking me up nor do

I remember my mom taking me to the hospital. All I knew was, I didn't realize what was happening to me.

In the psych unit, I heard for the first time the terms PTSD and Bipolar disorder. I was so embarrassed and ashamed it was hard to face anyone let alone those diagnoses. While in the psych unit, I was introduced to a counselor and a psychiatrist. I really wasn't interested in them. All I wanted at that point was to get out of the hospital and forget what just happened to me.

My parents didn't get involved at that time. I have no idea what they thought about the whole ordeal. They never mentioned it when I got out of the hospital like it never happened. Quite frankly I was happy they didn't mention it because I wanted to put it all behind me.

I did decide to continue counseling but went off of the medications shortly after I left the hospital. I guess being sober and not self-medicating was a bad mix. Needless to say, I wound up in a psych unit a second time a year later. This time was a nightmare.

Somehow the hospital thought I didn't have health insurance so they shipped me off to a Psychiatric Institute. The conditions were horrible.

Someone convinced my mom to visit. I don't know what she thought about my situation. It must have scared her because the next thing I knew my dad showed up and demanded to take me home. They weren't going to let me go but somehow, he checked me out of that place. On the ride home he told me I needed to do whatever it took to stop this from ever happening again.

A couple of days later I went to see my counselor. I remember telling him I was convinced it was PTSD that landed me back in the hospital again. At the time, I didn't realize the PTSD was driving my mania which led me to psychosis once more. I found myself more embarrassed and ashamed, and yet I still refused to believe I had bipolar disorder. I really believed it was my past trauma that was causing all my episodes.

I'd like to say I was well on my way to recovery because I was going to my counselor and working on my past issues, but I wound up back in a Psych unit again a year later.

After the third time, my main goal was to never wig out and wind up in a Psych unit again. I did whatever it took. I went through extensive counseling for many years. I researched PTSD to better understand what was happening to me. I paid attention to my mood swings, triggers, and anxiety before they got out of hand. I didn't want to stay up for days and wind up delusional again so I stayed away from caffeine. If I had trouble falling asleep, I'd take tranquilizers. If I was too anxious, I would take my anti-anxiety medication. Like I said, whatever it took I did. I never wanted to be unstable again. After the third stint of hospital stays, my mania and PTSD were controlled for years with anti-anxiety meds and tranquilizers.

My life began to get better slowly but surely. My relationships with my family and friends improved. My career in accounting took off. Life was good for many years.

In 1998 I fell in love and married a wonderful man. My husband Bart was the polar opposite of me. He was calm, quiet, and reserved. I was hyper, loud, and outgoing. I was very open with him about my PTSD and my past issues and he accepted that in me. He believed, as did I, that since it had been such a long time since I had wigged out, I didn't have to worry about those issues any longer. We just focused on our family life and careers.

That same year I started my accounting business. I worked 24/7 to get my business off the ground. He was very supportive and admired my ambitious nature.

My husband accepted all of my wild moods and my ideas. I remember one time when he was working the second shift, I had a bright idea to get rid of the carpeting in the whole house to reveal the old hardwood floors. I ripped it all out before he got home. I thought for sure he'd be upset but instead, he was just happy because all he had to do was throw out the carpet. He came home many nights finding major changes to the house. He never got mad. He said, "If it made me happy, he was fine with it." I think he was just happy he didn't have to do it. I was very fortunate to have a man like him. Most men would be furious.

For years, I juggled my marriage, the business, home remodeling projects, and household duties, took care of my in-law's health needs, and schooling, and taught classes at the college. I was always on the run.

I was living the dream. I had it all. I had a strong marriage and a supportive husband who put up with my mood swings and my blind ambition. My business was a success. Who could ask for more? But in 2013 I started burning out. I got physically and emotionally sick. I couldn't control my moods anymore. I would be angry one minute, sad the next minute then I was happy go lucky again. They were up and down and all over the place. I couldn't concentrate. I was weepy all the time. I started letting go of the business clients that caused me stress. I started getting triggered by flashbacks again from my past trauma. To top it off, I was diagnosed with autoimmune diseases.

To add to my stress, I had to find a new family physician that year because mine retired. During one of my doctor visits regarding my autoimmune diseases, I was crying and anxious. He made some recommendations regarding my behavior. I'll never forget, he said I needed to deal with the problem that is causing my behavior. He was implying I should go see a counselor to talk about my depression and a coo-coo doctor to get on medication. I was pissed. I didn't need a counselor or take any medications. I just had too much on my plate. I thought, who does he think he is telling me that? He doesn't know me. We just met not too long ago. I insisted that it was just the stress I was under causing all the health problems. He disagreed.

After that irritating visit, I knew deep down I needed help. I just didn't know for what. But I knew if I kept going the way that I did I would eventually wig out again. I just couldn't let that happen. I took half of his advice and called my counselor. It was time to face the music.

My Depressed Life

In the summer of 2013, I went back to see a counselor as my doctor recommended. I really was at a breaking point. I was having panic attacks and crying for days on end. I still refused any medications. In my mind, I felt that if I take any medication then I would have to admit I no longer had self-control. My ego and my pride would not allow it. I was ashamed once again that my life was out of control because of PTSD. I was livid this time.

During one of my counseling sessions, my therapist suggested I get on an anti-depressant. I wondered why she thought I was depressed. I thought, aren't most people who are depressed suicidal? I wasn't suicidal. I'm not depressed. However, unbeknownst to me, I had most of the symptoms of depression but was in total denial. I was weepy all the time. I felt hopeless and helpless. I no longer had the heart to run my business. I was tired all the time. I had panic attacks. But I was just too blind to see it.

Talking things out relieved enough pressure in order for me to function at a minimum. I decided to sell my business in September of that year. By doing that I thought I finally dealt with the issue that was causing all my problems. It took a lot off my plate but I was still dealing with the depression I conveniently denied.

One month later my husband Bart passed away from a massive heart attack. That event sent me down the darkest path I have ever faced in my life. My world shattered the moment he took his last breath.

Honestly, I wanted to die. I had nothing to live for. I sold my business and now my husband, my future was gone. I have to be honest, if my sister and brother didn't show up at the hospital that night, I would have succeeded in ending my life. I already had a plan in my head for that.

The first couple of days were rough. I cried constantly and I couldn't sleep. I had a close friend of mine come and take the guns out of my house that way it wouldn't be easy for me to pull the trigger. My sister, my brother, and my dearest friend never left my side for fear I would kill myself or wig out. I was on the verge of both. I truly believe they saved my life. They stayed with me for months until I showed signs that I was ok to be on my own. It had to be hard on them to see me in such despair.

Once everybody went back to their normal lives, I had to face my depression alone. I found myself sleeping days and weeks away hoping my autoimmune diseases would kill me. They didn't. I prayed that God would take me. He didn't.

Since dying wasn't happening, I started getting up and taking on small projects around the house to keep me busy since I wasn't working any longer. Then I started taking on bigger home remodels. My mania kicked in. I started spending money like there was no tomorrow. No amount of money could repair my grief.

About a year after Bart's death, I could no longer control my extreme highs and lows. I was up for days and paranoid when the psychosis set in for the fourth time. And of course, I jumped in my car and drove aimlessly around. I wound up at a friend's house. They knew something wasn't right. They took me home and stayed with me. Thank God my sister called while they were there. She came right over and called my brother and my best friend.

What they saw was a nonresponsive delusional individual. To the best of their abilities, they tried to help. They had no choice other than to call the Sheriff and the Paramedics. I don't remember whether the sheriff arrived when the paramedics did. However, I was told that I would not go with the paramedics. That's when the sheriff escorted me to the hospital. I found myself in a psych unit once more.

Denial is a comfort when you are not ready to face the truth. I still believed it was PTSD, not bipolar disorder causing these episodes. But I began to feel defeated.

For years after that stint in the hospital, I cycled from depression to mania. I was on a roller coaster ride I just couldn't get off of.

When I was depressed, I went to concerts, movies, plays, parties and went out to dinner with friends. I even tried dating which ended in disaster. Bought a pool and had pool parties all summer but nothing brought me joy. I hated the world and I hated to be in it.

When I was manic, I'd spend money like I was the wealthiest person in the world. I'd take on many projects around the house and stay up all night getting them done.

After six years of faking my happiness, I decided to get on anti-depressant medication. I was miserable and I was willing to try anything to make my life brighter. Who knew what a change might do?

The funny thing is through all that I still didn't believe my depression had anything to do with bipolar disorder. I just thought I was stuck in my grief from the loss of my husband. Crazy Huh!

Acceptance

My road to acceptance was a long and bumpy ride. Knowing about bipolar and accepting your diagnosis are two different things. Maybe part of my denial was the fact I never really knew exactly what bipolar was. I thought my behavior was normal for me. I was just different from others. That's not a bad thing.

I knew deep down something wasn't quite right but I was just not ready to face the truth. As I stated in the previous chapters I was in denial for years. I thought I was strong enough to handle things on my own. Plus, I didn't think I was that bad even though I had been in a psych unit four times already.

After the fourth stint in the psych unit, a light began to come on. Not completely but was there since they had put me on an anti-psychotic medication that actually helped me. My mind slowed down. My thought processes were better. The talking wildly stopped. The sleepless nights stopped. The spending was under control. I thought maybe, just maybe I have bipolar.

I stayed on the medication for about three months after I was released from the hospital. I got off it because I gained 50 lbs. I just could not deal with that. It was bad enough I felt ashamed and helpless and depressed but to add that kind of weight so quickly made me feel worse.

I was feeling pretty good for quite some time. I even decided I would go to a bipolar support group to see if I fit in. I went to two meetings. I didn't learn a lot about bipolar. However, the one thing I gathered was you would have to be medicated for the rest of your life. Taking medication for life was not for me. I left and never looked back.

I stayed off medication for several years after that time. I swung from mania to depression constantly. I finally got to a point where I was out of control and afraid. Afraid that I was going to wind up back in the hospital. That's when I called my psychiatrist.

I told him my PTSD was kicking in again and I needed help. He prescribed me another antipsychotic medication. I thought the medication was for controlling my hypervigilance, in all actuality it was controlling my mania.

I took those meds for about a year. My life got better. I wasn't talking wildly or spending carelessly or staying up for days on end. But I found myself more depressed. I still struggled with worthlessness, and sadness and I wanted to die.

I talked to my doctor again and this time I was ready to deal with my depression. He put me on a different antidepressant medication that turned my life around. For the first time in my life, I felt normal in my own skin.

I still didn't believe I had bipolar. I thought the mania was hypervigilance from PTSD. As for the depression, I thought it was from being stuck in my grief from the loss of my husband.

All in all, for about two years, life was very good for me. But unfortunately, I started getting tremors in my hands and head. I started dragging my right foot and tripping on everything and my cognitive abilities were diminishing. The doctor thought it might be a side effect of the antipsychotic medication I was on.

I went to a neurologist to see what was going on. He said it could be Parkinsonism from the medication or Parkinson's Disease. To know for sure what it is I'd either have to go on a different type of medicine or get the medicine out of my system for six months.

I was doing really well emotionally. I didn't think it would hurt to go off my meds for too long. I needed to know if I had Parkinson's or not. I chose to go off my medication for six months in order to know for sure; to confirm.

That was the beginning of the end of my denial for me. I was good for about two months. Then the weepiness kicked in. The obsessive thoughts crept in. The excessive talking began. The sleepless nights worked their way back. The spending started up again. My family and friends were telling me I needed to get back on my medication because my behavior was off the hook. Unfortunately after going through all that, my tremors and all the other symptoms that went with them didn't go away.

Six months off the medication I was diagnosed with Parkinson's Disease. My stress level went through the roof and my mania kicked in even higher. I decided at that moment I was going to live my life to the fullest until I can't. I decided to sell my house and go to Florida for six months.

After I sold my house and moved to Florida, my family, and friends still tried to convince me that I was acting manic and I needed to get back on my medication. I just kept saying it was from the stress. I can handle it. I didn't want to make my Parkinson's worse with the medication. I chose my physical well-being over my mental well-being at that time. That decision cost me my mental state and almost cost me my relationship with my sister.

I was only in Florida for two months when the sleepless nights and delusions set in. In my delusion, I thought I needed to sacrifice myself in order to keep my sister safe. I got in my car with my dog and started to drive. I drove back to Ohio to my sister's house. I really don't remember the road trip other than I did make it to a hotel the first night. When she asked me what I was doing there I really didn't know. I was talking irrationally. They had to call the Sherriff to escort me to the hospital because they were afraid of what I might do to myself. Thank God her family was able to convince me to go. I can't imagine how she felt seeing me like that and hearing all the delusional thoughts I was saying and having to call the Sherriff for help.

Now here I am in the hospital yet again for the fifth time. I couldn't keep putting myself or my family through this kind of trauma anymore. It was time to face the truth. But what was the truth?

I'd like to say I believed I was bipolar at that point but I still fought the diagnosis. This time I was even angrier. Angry because I couldn't control it. Angry because yes, I do need medication to help with my mental state. Angry because I hurt so many people with my behavior that I couldn't control. Angry because I was less than perfect.

I needed answers. I decided to research PTSD again to see what I was missing. I read many books, and articles and went on websites to understand all the symptoms and treatments for PTSD. The doctors were right in diagnosing me with PTSD.

However, I had other symptoms that didn't fall under that diagnosis. Maybe, just maybe he was right about me having bipolar.

Next, I decided to research bipolar disorder. When I did the light came on completely. I never really understood what they meant by being bipolar. Like I said over and over again all I heard in my mind is that you are crazy. But when I read about all the symptoms and honestly looked back at my life, I was ashamed that I denied it for so long.

I put the people I love the most through a tremendous amount of pain. Watching me crash and burn many times just because of the shame and the stigma behind the word Bipolar. I don't ever want to do that to myself or them again.

I will take my medication for my mental well-being just as I do for my physical well-being.

Medication and Me

I could not end this short story without talking about the other reason why I ran from the bipolar diagnosis. It was the fear of losing my mind on medication. The fear came from the first time I was ever medicated, I had the worst experience from the side effects.

The first time I was in the psychiatric unit, they gave me high doses of Haldol, Cogentin, and Lithium. I guess for some patients that works but for me, it was a nightmare. I felt drunk and disorientated, my skin crawled, my whole body shook with tremors and I became suicidal. I don't know which medicine caused all of the side effects.

I remember calling my therapist. I was frantic. I said, "I didn't get sober to find myself on medication that makes me feel drunk and disorientated all day. Nor did I get on medication to come up with ten ways to kill myself." I demanded him to take me off the medication. Of course, you can't just stop that type of medicine. You have to gradually reduce the dose. It was the worst three weeks of my life. I never wanted to feel that way again.

From that experience, I fought all bipolar medication for years. When I was under a doctor's care, I would take anti-anxiety or antidepressants but not anti-psychotics. When I went to the hospital, I would take what they gave me and go off them when I was released.

The fourth time I wigged out and wound up in the hospital I was fortunate enough to get a doctor that actually listened to me instead of dismissing me. He asked me why I didn't want to take medicine and what was I afraid of. Maybe I was getting tired or defeated but

I shared with him my first experience with medication.

He then took a different approach with me. He put me on the lowest dose of an antipsychotic medication. It really helped me for the first time in my life. I stayed on it when I left the hospital. I took it for about three months. But as I stated in the previous chapter, I gained 50 lbs. and I wasn't going to deal with weight gain. Plus, I was feeling good. I didn't think I needed my medication anymore.

One good thing is my doctor respected my decision to go off the medication. He didn't lecture or pressure me. He listened to my concerns. However, he did encourage me to stick to my appointments in order for him to monitor my anxiety and depression. I stuck with him

A couple of years after I quit taking the medicine I was struggling with weepiness, mood swings, obsessive thoughts, and spending money again. I asked my doctor for help. He knew my concerns about weight gain. That's when he prescribed an anti-psychotic that had fewer side effects and started me off on the lowest dose. It helped me considerably. I stayed on that medication up to the time I went off it to get a clear diagnosis of Parkinson's disease.

It's unfortunate that I had to go through one more stint in the hospital to finally realize I needed to be medicated for life.

Getting on medicine and staying on the medicine is a big adjustment. I had to learn to be still and be comfortable with that. However, that learning process was very difficult for me. I was always busy non-stop. I thought if I wasn't moving, I was being lazy. I felt guilty and I felt useless. I stuck with it though. In my stillness I learned how to make plans, actually listen to conversations without interrupting, and get things accomplished without all the stress and anxiety.

I am very grateful my psychiatrist could see right through my denial. He handled my denial rather well. He gave me the time to come to my own conclusions about my diagnosis.

My advice to anyone struggling with bipolar disorder is to find a psychiatrist who really cares and listens.

Life Today

It's been over a year since my last stint in a psych unit. Acceptance, counseling, and medication have truly changed my life. I have my eyes wide open now. I know I will never be cured but it can be managed.

I have good days and bad days just not to the extremes that they use to be. I have to manage my stress because it is a big trigger for me.

I thought I would miss being manic, but spinning my wheels and pushing to get things done as fast as possible does not appeal to me anymore. I like slow and steady. Taking time to do things right. Not feeling completely exhausted and anxious for pushing so hard.

I don't miss all the crazy ways I handled relationships. Jumping in because it felt good at the time and waking up to the reality of my behavior. I lived in shame for years because I couldn't control my thoughts or behavior.

I like being able to hold a thought in my head instead of bouncing from idea to idea without fully being able to think things through.

I like being able to make healthy choices where money is concerned. I no longer have to suffer the consequences of poor choices

I enjoy having a decent conversation with someone without getting overstimulated by the conversation or bouncing from subject to subject.

I love being able to have a good night's sleep because my mind no longer races throughout the night.

I am feeling blessed that I am no longer depressed. I don't miss those feelings of hopelessness, helplessness, unworthiness, weepiness, or wanting to die.

I have found joy in the little things in life like walking my dog at the park. I really am happy to be alive today.

I am grateful that I have a great psychiatrist. I am confident that if my behavior starts to change, he will be there to help. He has not steered me wrong yet.

I am most grateful that I have supportive family and friends that love and accept me for who and how I am.

I know throughout my life I ran from the diagnosis of bipolar and suffered many consequences because I didn't want to be labeled crazy. The funny thing about the way I lived my life and living in denial all those years was crazy. I really don't ever want to go back to that way of life.

Accepting the diagnosis of bipolar disorder does not define me. I am not ashamed anymore. I am not bipolar. I have bipolar. It's just a mental disorder that I have that needs to be treated just like my Parkinson's does. That I will never forget.